I0392673

Advertising 101

Learning the aspects of Advertising

Daniel A. Garcia

Dedication

This is Dedicated to all of my family and friends in Las Cruces, NM. Along with everyone involved in advertising.

Go Get 'EM!

How To Use

This is a very interactive Journal. This Journal will help you stay on the right track when it comes to advertising.

This Journal is made up of the following:

• Critical Questions- to help your development of Print, Billboard, and Social Media Ads.

• Check List- Keep track of progress.

• Note Section- to make note of progress and/or fulfilment of a particular Ad.

In your creation of Ads, this journal serves as a guide to build a foundation, in which you can advertise with confidence after completing this journal.

Print Ad

Print Ads can be a lot of fun. They allow someone like you and I to make the best use of a picture and/or wording to send a memorable message.

Print Ads are the "origin" or "traditional form" of advertising. In the sense that they are found in magazines, business catalogs, newspapers, newsletters, or anything else that is printed.

Use the following layout of questions to help sharpen your skills.

Print Ad # _____ Date: _____

❑ What is the usage of white space? Is it used up by pictures and/or wording?

_____

_____

_____

_____

❑ Is there a Message? What is it?

_____

_____

_____

_____

❑ Does the Ad make sense? Is it Memorable?

_____

_____

_____

_____

❑ When people think of a product, do they think of your Ad? Or store?

_____

_____

_____

_____

Print Ad # _____ Date: _____

❑ What is the usage of white space? Is it used up by
   pictures and/or wording?

_____

_____

_____

_____

❑ Is there a Message? What is it?

_____

_____

_____

_____

❑ Does the Ad make sense? Is it Memorable?

_____

_____

_____

_____

❑ When people think of a product, do they think of
   your Ad? Or store?

_____

_____

_____

_____

Print Ad # _____ Date: _____

❏ What is the usage of white space? Is it used up by pictures and/or wording?

_____

_____

_____

_____

❏ Is there a Message? What is it?

_____

_____

_____

_____

❏ Does the Ad make sense? Is it Memorable?

_____

_____

_____

_____

❏ When people think of a product, do they think of your Ad? Or store?

_____

_____

_____

_____

Print Ad # _____ Date: _____

☐ What is the usage of white space? Is it used up by
  pictures and/or wording?

_____

_____

_____

_____

☐ Is there a Message? What is it?

_____

_____

_____

_____

☐ Does the Ad make sense? Is it Memorable?

_____

_____

_____

_____

☐ When people think of a product, do they think of
  your Ad? Or store?

_____

_____

_____

_____

Print Ad # _____ Date: _____

☐ What is the usage of white space? Is it used up by pictures and/or wording?

_____

_____

_____

_____

☐ Is there a Message? What is it?

_____

_____

_____

_____

☐ Does the Ad make sense? Is it Memorable?

_____

_____

_____

_____

☐ When people think of a product, do they think of your Ad? Or store?

_____

_____

_____

_____

Print Ad # _____ Date: _____

❑ What is the usage of white space? Is it used up by
pictures and/or wording?

_____

_____

_____

_____

❑ Is there a Message? What is it?

_____

_____

_____

_____

❑ Does the Ad make sense? Is it Memorable?

_____

_____

_____

_____

❑ When people think of a product, do they think of
your Ad? Or store?

_____

_____

_____

_____

Print Ad # _____ Date: _____

☐ What is the usage of white space? Is it used up by pictures and/or wording?

_____

_____

_____

_____

☐ Is there a Message? What is it?

_____

_____

_____

_____

☐ Does the Ad make sense? Is it Memorable?

_____

_____

_____

_____

☐ When people think of a product, do they think of your Ad? Or store?

_____

_____

_____

_____

Print Ad # _____ Date: _____

❑ What is the usage of white space? Is it used up by
   pictures and/or wording?

_____

_____

_____

_____

❑ Is there a Message? What is it?

_____

_____

_____

_____

❑ Does the Ad make sense? Is it Memorable?

_____

_____

_____

_____

❑ When people think of a product, do they think of
   your Ad? Or store?

_____

_____

_____

_____

Print Ad # _____ Date: _____

☐ What is the usage of white space? Is it used up by pictures and/or wording?

_____

_____

_____

_____

☐ Is there a Message? What is it?

_____

_____

_____

_____

☐ Does the Ad make sense? Is it Memorable?

_____

_____

_____

_____

☐ When people think of a product, do they think of your Ad? Or store?

_____

_____

_____

_____

Billboard Ad

Billboard Ads are very unique, it gives advertisers another canvas to use. I mean what else are we going to look at while driving? Lol.

Billboard Ads are viewed at a quick rate, so the message should be clear, readable, and memorable all within a couple of seconds. Most Billboard Ads are emotional pictures, that make up majority of the white space. So this should be a fun experience for you!

Use the following layout of questions to help sharpen your skills.

Billboard Ad # _____   Date: _____

❑ What is the usage of white space? Is it used up by pictures and/or wording?

_____

_____

_____

_____

❑ Is there a Message? What is it?

_____

_____

_____

_____

❑ Does the Ad make sense? Is it Memorable?

_____

_____

_____

_____

❑ When people think of a product, do they think of your Ad? Or store?

_____

_____

_____

_____

Billboard Ad # _____   Date: _____

❑ What is the usage of white space? Is it used up by pictures and/or wording?

_____

_____

_____

_____

❑ Is there a Message? What is it?

_____

_____

_____

_____

❑ Does the Ad make sense? Is it Memorable?

_____

_____

_____

_____

❑ When people think of a product, do they think of your Ad? Or store?

_____

_____

_____

_____

Billboard Ad # _____ Date: _____

❑ What is the usage of white space? Is it used up by pictures and/or wording?

_____

_____

_____

_____

❑ Is there a Message? What is it?

_____

_____

_____

_____

❑ Does the Ad make sense? Is it Memorable?

_____

_____

_____

_____

❑ When people think of a product, do they think of your Ad? Or store?

_____

_____

_____

_____

Billboard Ad # _____   Date: _____

❑ What is the usage of white space? Is it used up by
   pictures and/or wording?

_____

_____

_____

_____

❑ Is there a Message? What is it?

_____

_____

_____

_____

❑ Does the Ad make sense? Is it Memorable?

_____

_____

_____

_____

❑ When people think of a product, do they think of
   your Ad? Or store?

_____

_____

_____

_____

Billboard Ad # _____   Date: _____

❏ What is the usage of white space? Is it used up by pictures and/or wording?

_____

_____

_____

_____

❏ Is there a Message? What is it?

_____

_____

_____

_____

❏ Does the Ad make sense? Is it Memorable?

_____

_____

_____

_____

❏ When people think of a product, do they think of your Ad? Or store?

_____

_____

_____

_____

Billboard Ad # _____   Date: _____

❏ What is the usage of white space? Is it used up by pictures and/or wording?

_____

_____

_____

_____

❏ Is there a Message? What is it?

_____

_____

_____

❏ Does the Ad make sense? Is it Memorable?

_____

_____

_____

_____

❏ When people think of a product, do they think of your Ad? Or store?

_____

_____

_____

_____

Billboard Ad # _____ Date: _____

❑ What is the usage of white space? Is it used up by pictures and/or wording?

_____

_____

_____

_____

❑ Is there a Message? What is it?

_____

_____

_____

_____

❑ Does the Ad make sense? Is it Memorable?

_____

_____

_____

_____

❑ When people think of a product, do they think of your Ad? Or store?

_____

_____

_____

_____

Billboard Ad # _____   Date: _____

❑ What is the usage of white space? Is it used up by pictures and/or wording?

_____

_____

_____

_____

❑ Is there a Message? What is it?

_____

_____

_____

_____

❑ Does the Ad make sense? Is it Memorable?

_____

_____

_____

_____

❑ When people think of a product, do they think of your Ad? Or store?

_____

_____

_____

_____

Billboard Ad # _____   Date: _____

❑ What is the usage of white space? Is it used up by pictures and/or wording?

_____

_____

_____

_____

❑ Is there a Message? What is it?

_____

_____

_____

_____

❑ Does the Ad make sense? Is it Memorable?

_____

_____

_____

_____

❑ When people think of a product, do they think of your Ad? Or store?

_____

_____

_____

_____

Social Media Ad

Social Media today has become a massive outlet to share or in this case advertise your business and/or product with the world-wide web.

Since this is such a game changer it makes it easy for someone like you and I to advertise for free! So the sky is the limit for your ideas to come into fruition.

Use the following layout of questions to help sharpen your skills.

Social Media Ad # _____   Date: _____

❑ What is the usage of white space? Is it used up by pictures and/or wording?

_____

_____

_____

_____

❑ Is there a Message? What is it?

_____

_____

_____

_____

❑ Does the Ad make sense? Is it Memorable?

_____

_____

_____

_____

❑ When people think of a product, do they think of your Ad? Or store?

_____

_____

_____

_____

Social Media Ad # _____   Date: _____

☐ What is the usage of white space? Is it used up by pictures and/or wording?

_____

_____

_____

_____

☐ Is there a Message? What is it?

_____

_____

_____

_____

☐ Does the Ad make sense? Is it Memorable?

_____

_____

_____

_____

☐ When people think of a product, do they think of your Ad? Or store?

_____

_____

_____

_____

Social Media Ad # _____   Date: _____

❑ What is the usage of white space? Is it used up by pictures and/or wording?

_____

_____

_____

_____

❑ Is there a Message? What is it?

_____

_____

_____

_____

❑ Does the Ad make sense? Is it Memorable?

_____

_____

_____

_____

❑ When people think of a product, do they think of your Ad? Or store?

_____

_____

_____

_____

Social Media Ad # _____   Date: _____

❑ What is the usage of white space? Is it used up by pictures and/or wording?

_____

_____

_____

_____

❑ Is there a Message? What is it?

_____

_____

_____

_____

❑ Does the Ad make sense? Is it Memorable?

_____

_____

_____

_____

❑ When people think of a product, do they think of your Ad? Or store?

_____

_____

_____

_____

Social Media Ad # _____ Date:_____

❑ What is the usage of white space? Is it used up by pictures and/or wording?

_____

_____

_____

_____

❑ Is there a Message? What is it?

_____

_____

_____

_____

❑ Does the Ad make sense? Is it Memorable?

_____

_____

_____

_____

❑ When people think of a product, do they think of your Ad? Or store?

_____

_____

_____

_____

Social Media Ad # _____ Date: _____

❑ What is the usage of white space? Is it used up by pictures and/or wording?

_____
_____
_____
_____

❑ Is there a Message? What is it?

_____
_____
_____
_____

❑ Does the Ad make sense? Is it Memorable?

_____
_____
_____
_____

❑ When people think of a product, do they think of your Ad? Or store?

_____
_____
_____
_____

Social Media Ad # _____   Date: _____

❑ What is the usage of white space? Is it used up by pictures and/or wording?

_____

_____

_____

_____

❑ Is there a Message? What is it?

_____

_____

_____

_____

❑ Does the Ad make sense? Is it Memorable?

_____

_____

_____

_____

❑ When people think of a product, do they think of your Ad? Or store?

_____

_____

_____

_____

Social Media Ad # _____   Date: _____

❑ What is the usage of white space? Is it used up by pictures and/or wording?

_____

_____

_____

_____

❑ Is there a Message? What is it?

_____

_____

_____

_____

❑ Does the Ad make sense? Is it Memorable?

_____

_____

_____

_____

❑ When people think of a product, do they think of your Ad? Or store?

_____

_____

_____

_____

Social Media Ad # _____ Date: _____

❑ What is the usage of white space? Is it used up by pictures and/or wording?

_____

_____

_____

_____

❑ Is there a Message? What is it?

_____

_____

_____

_____

❑ Does the Ad make sense? Is it Memorable?

_____

_____

_____

_____

❑ When people think of a product, do they think of your Ad? Or store?

_____

_____

_____

_____

Advertising is so essential for any business owner to possess. Your future may very well depend on it, advertising is really about making your potential customer(s) remember you, so they can come in and buy your product(s).

Thank You for purchasing this Journal. Please keep a look out for others.

Best Wishes,
Daniel A. Garcia